Dog Trick

15 Tricks You Must Teach Your Dog before Anything Else

Your Free Gift

As a way of thanking you for the purchase, I'd like to offer you a complimentary gift:

- **5 Pillar Life Transformation Checklist:** This short book is about life transformation, presented in bit size pieces for easy implementation. I believe that without such a checklist, you are likely to have a hard time implementing anything in this book and any other thing you set out to do religiously and sticking to it for the long haul. It doesn't matter whether your goals relate to weight loss, relationships, personal finance, investing, personal development, improving communication in your family, your overall health, finances, improving your sex life, resolving issues in your relationship, fighting PMS successfully, investing, running a successful business, traveling etc. With a checklist like this one, you can bet that anything you do will seem a lot easier to implement until the end. Therefore, even if you don't continue reading this book, at least read the one thing that will help you in every other aspect of your life. Grab your copy now by clicking/tapping here or simply enter http://bit.ly/2fantonfreebie into your browser. Your life will never be the same again (if you implement what's in this book), I promise.

PS: I'd like your feedback. If you are happy with this book, please leave a review on Amazon.

Introduction

Have you seen one of those dogs that seamlessly do whatever their owner tells them to do and wondered, *"God, how did he manage to teach him how to do that?"*

Have you wished that you could teach your dog to do the same? If so, then this book is perfect for you.

This book will show you a number of exciting tricks that you can teach your dog. In this amazing book, you will find step-by-step instructions on how you can train your dog a number of cool tricks. This book will guide you on what you need to do every step of the way. You are never left wondering what to do next. Think of it as your personal dog training bible.

The tricks covered in this book range from relatively simple ones to the more advanced. By the time you are done covering the material in this book, you will have made your dog sharper and smarter than you could have imagined. You will be amazed at your dog's new ability to do things once given a simple command.

Are you excited about this? If so, then let's begin.

Table of Contents

We will begin our discussion by looking at basic tricks first. These are tricks that will require minimal input from you in terms of effort and time. They are also easy for your dog to learn since they involve relatively simple steps. Therefore, you are likely to experience less difficulty teaching them to your dog.

Basic Tricks

Trick 1: Sit

Difficulty: Basic

What you will need: A treat

Amount of time needed: Around 10 minutes, 2 to 3 times in a day

The first trick that you will need to teach your dog is that of sitting on command. This happens to be one of the easiest tricks that can be taught to a dog, so you shouldn't have a lot of trouble with this one. However, you will still need to follow a number of steps for your dog to master this command. In truth, there are a many ways to go about training your dog on how to sit. In this chapter, I will teach you a method that is my personal favorite.

Step 1: Get a treat

The first step is that of getting treats to use. Nearly every dog-training exercise will involve using treats, so acquiring them beforehand is a crucial first step. Also, remember to acquire treats that are small in size. The frequency of using treats to train your dog means that you should stay away from using huge treats; otherwise; you run the risk of over-feeding your dog.

Step 2: Get the attention of your dog

Next, you will need to get the full attention of your dog. You can do this by standing directly in front of your dog. If your dog faces you this way, it will be difficult for him or her to be distracted, which will then improve the quality of your training.

Step 3: Hold the treat in your hand

After that, hold the treat in your hand and show it to the dog. Show it to him or her but do not let him or her have it. Now your dog will be fully aware that you have a treat in your possession and will be fully focused on ways of acquiring it. At this point, your dog will be open to doing anything to get the treat, which paves way for you to start giving lessons.

Step 4: Move the treat around

Now it's time to move your hand around so that your dog follows it. You can move it closer to the dog's nose and behind the head. The goal in this step is to get your dog in a sitting position. Pay attention to how close you are holding the treat. Don't hold the treat too high since this will make the dog jump. Also, don't hold it too low, which can make the dog stand instead. Adjust the position accordingly, depending on the height of your dog.

Step 5: Say the word 'sit'

As your dog tries to get into a sitting position, it's time to start using the word 'sit'. This step is very important because this will be the command you will tend to use every time you want to put your dog down to a sitting position.

Step 6: Give the dog the treat

At this point, if your dog is seated in the right position, as you would want, it's time to reward him or her with the treat. Remember to hand the treat right from your hand so that your dog won't have to adjust his or her position to consume the treat.

Step 7: Congratulate the dog

To wrap things up, you will need to congratulate your dog for behaving accordingly. A simple "Good boy or girl" should suffice at this point. You can also rub his or her head to send the message that he or she behaved in a way that you liked. To release your dog from this position, you can take a step back so that he or she is prompted to come over towards you.

After performing the steps above, the trick is to keep repeating these exercises from time to time. As a rule, you should go over these steps three times a day. If you keep doing this, it will only be a while before your dog starts responding to this command. After a week or so, you can withdraw the treat and start using the command without using a treat. If your dog doesn't respond, accordingly, try alternating the use of treats with not using. After some time, your dog will start obeying the command even without treats.

One thing to remember however is the command that you use. Trying to mix up words won't work well. For instance, saying "come on sit" or "no sit" is not ideal. This can end up confusing your dog instead. Being specific by saying "sit" works better.

Now that you have learnt the first trick, let's move on to the next one, "Shaking."

Trick 2: Shake

Difficulty: Basic

What you will need: A few treats

Time needed: Around 5 minutes, two to three times in a day

Would you like your dog to greet you or your friends with the paws every time he or she is told to? Teaching your dog how to shake can accomplish that. Also, teaching your dog how to shake is important because it sets the foundation for other tricks that follow such as waving. Waving will be covered in the next chapter. In the meantime, your attention needs to be devoted to teaching your dog how to shake. The purpose of this trick is to show you how to teach your dog how to shake hands with its paws.

Step 1: Make your dog sit

This is important for this trick to work. Your dog needs to know how to sit when given the command. The previous trick covered this. If you haven't taught your dog yet how to do this, then you need to revisit the previous trick and work through the material provided there. After you do that, then you can go to the next step.

Step 2: Hold a treat in your hand

The next step is to hold a treat in your hand and close your fist. At first, you can show it to your dog, but don't let him or her have it. Close your fist to ensure this. This is meant to attract the attention of your dog. Your dog will try to figure out ways to get this treat. One way would be trying to stand. Once he or she does that, give the command "sit" to get him or her back to her sitting position.

Step 3: Use the command "shake"

At this point, it's time to start using the command "shake." As you do this, your dog will attempt to raise its paw in an attempt to get the treat hidden in your hand. This is something most dogs will do instinctively once the standing attempt fails. If your dog starts raising its paws as you say the word "shake," it's time to prepare yourself for the next step.

Step 4: Offer your dog the treat

If your dog is responding well by raising its paw, it is time to give your reward. This is where your treat comes in. As you offer your dog the treat, you can hold the paw with one hand as you offer the treat with the other hand. The point of this is to make your dog get that the point of this command is to shake your hand. The treat is merely a reward for acting accordingly.

Step 5: Congratulate your dog

If your dog has responded appropriately through the steps that we've gone though, it's a good practice to congratulate it. You could try saying "good boy or girl" or a simple "yes" enthusiastically. Your dog will notice your energy and excitement and will likely offer its paw the next time you issue the command "shake."

The steps up to this point need to be repeated two or three times in a day for about a week. If your dog is responding well to these steps with consistency, it is time to remove the treat from the exercises.

Step 6: Removing the treat.

Removing the treat from the exercises is important because in the future, you will not always offer a treat every time you ask your dog to shake your hand. So after the first week, you can start alternating periods of treats with those without treats as a way of easing your dog into the idea of shaking hands without expecting a treat in return.

As time goes, your dog should respond well every time you issue the command shake, even without the use of a treat, if you follow the steps we have discussed thus far. If you see this, then you should be certain that your dog has learnt the trick and it is time to teach him or her yet another trick, waving

Trick 3: Wave

Difficulty: Basic-Intermediate**

Note:

The reason this intermediate trick is here is because it builds on the previous trick. I saw it fit to have it here instead of having it in the intermediate tricks category for easy learning.

What you will need: A few treats

Amount of time needed: Around 10 minutes, three times a day

Could you imagine your dog raising its hand to wave at you or your friends as a way of greeting? How cool is that? Many are the times we have come across dogs that jump to greet the owner or visitors. Such behavior is risky and undesirable. Instead, it would be better if you trained your dog to wave instead. It is more disciplined and your friends will be impressed to say the least.

This trick will show you the steps you can use to teach your dog how to wave.

Step 1: Make sure that your dog knows how to shake

One thing you need to know about the "wave" trick is that it is slightly advanced. Because of this, one prerequisite to teaching your dog this trick is that it must have learnt how to shake. The trick of waving builds up on what your dog already knows, in this case shaking.

In the previous trick, we covered this. If your dog hasn't learnt this trick yet, it is time that you revisited the previous trick and covered the material before we take any step further.

Step 2: Get your dog in a sitting position and give the "shake" command

After you are certain that your dog has fully learnt the shake trick, it is time to make him or her sit in front of you by issuing the "sit" command that we learnt in the first trick. Then, once your dog sits, give the command "shake". If your dog already knows this command, it should raise one of its paws. Now it's time for the next step.

Step 3: Raise your hand a bit higher

If your dog has already raised one of his or her paws, you should take things a little bit further. Instead of accepting the greeting as you would if you were shaking, you should raise your hand a bit higher so that your dog tries to reach for it by raising his or her paw higher in return. The whole point in this exercise is to ensure that your dog raises his or her paw slightly above the head.

Step 4: Issue the command "wave"

As your dog raises its paw above its head as tries to reach your hand, you should issue the command "wave". This is meant to train the dog to associate this action with this command. You could also try whatever command you prefer. For instance, saying "say hello" or "wave bye" are good alternatives. However, remember to be consistent with whatever command that you choose to use, to avoid confusing your dog.

Step 4: Congratulate your dog and hand it a treat

If your dog has responded appropriately without standing or jumping, it is time to reward the good behavior. As a rule, giving a treat and following it with praise is a good way to go about this. It communicates to the dog that he or she has behaved accordingly and increases the likelihood of he or she will learn faster.

Step 5: Stop using the command "shake" and stick with "wave" instead.

After your dog starts showing some consistency with the steps above for like three or four days, you should stop using the command "shake". Start using the command "wave" exclusively and see how your dog responds. If he doesn't respond well, go over the steps above once more until your dog shows some consistency.

Step 6: Start issuing treats only for the best waves

Now it is time to start reserving your treats only for the best waves. Check to see for instances when your dog has raised his or her paw above her head and moving it in an up and down fashion. Only then should you offer your treat.

Step 7: Phase out the treats

If your dog starts showing a good follow through in the steps covered, it is time to start alternating periods of treats with periods of no treats and proceed to removing treats from your commands entirely.

To conclude, waving is one of the neatest tricks you can teach your dog. It offers your dog a nice way of interacting with you and other people in a manner that is calm and controlled. It is slightly advanced but with a bit of patience and persistence, you should get it right. If learnt properly, your dog will easily charm you and your guests with its pleasant and obedient behavior.

That said, it is time to move to the next trick in line, teaching your dog to lie down.

Trick 4: Lie Down

Difficulty: Easy

What you will need: A treat

Amount of time needed: Around 10 minutes, 2 to 3 times in a day

So you have taught your dog a number of tricks including: sitting, shaking, and waving. But what if you wanted your dog to be able to lie on the ground when you want him to, and stay there until you release him? Can you picture your dog being that obedient? Well apparently, training him to do that is not as hard as you may think.

In this chapter, you will learn how to teach your dog to lie down when told to. So, whether you want your dog to relax after a long day or make him or her stick around for a long period, you should read this chapter to find out.

Step 1: Get a nice treat

In all likelihood, you will always need a treat to train your dog and this instance is no exception. So to begin, find out what type of treat is your dog's favorite and acquire it before anything else. Also, make sure that your treat is of small size so that you avoid over-feeding your dog.

Step 2: Get your dog's attention

The next step is that of getting your dog's attention. One great and easy way to this is to simply show your dog the treat. This is an instant attention grabber in any situation. You can move it close to your dog's nose so that he or she sniffs it and becomes more anxious. At this point, you can be sure that you have your dog's full attention and can proceed with the next steps:

Step 3: Make your dog sit

Now that you have your dog's full attention, it is time that you put him or her at a sitting position. A quick way to do this is to issue the sit command. At this point, your dog should have known the sit command and gotten used to it. If you haven't trained your dog on this trick, go to the first chapter and start from there. If your dog already knows it, read on.

Step 4: Bring the treat close to your dog and use the lie command

With your dog in a sitting position, it is time to show the treat to your dog. Show it to your dog but do not offer it to him or her yet. As you do this, start issuing the command "lie." You can try using "lie down," "down," "lie" or some variation of that. This is the point where you start teaching him or her to associate the command with act of lying down.

Step 6: Beckon your dog to a "down" position.

Now it is time to guide your dog to a down position. To do this, simply hold the treat close to your dog's face but at a safe distance that he or she can't just reach out and grab it. Then slowly, bring it down closer to the ground. Your dog should follow the treat to the ground. As he or she does that, you can hold him or her down gently with your hand to stop him from getting back up.

Step 7: Offer your treat and praise

Once you have confirmed that your dog's belly, rear end and elbows are touching the floor, offer him or her the treat. As you do this, also remember to shower your dog with praise and a small pat on the head as a signal that he or she did something good. This works well to reinforce the lesson. One thing to remember though is that you should only offer your dog a treat once he or she is in a down position. If your dog gets back up, withdraw the treat and go over the steps from the first one once again.

Step 8: Release your dog from this position

After your dog has gone through the steps above successfully and is still lying on the ground, it is time to release him or her. A simple way to do this is to simply take a step back and clap your hands. This should prompt your dog to come over to you effectively releasing him from his position. You can even try giving the command "up" or "ok" as you do his so that your dog relates being released with this command.

As you can see, training your dog to lie on the ground is not a difficult task. By simply wielding a nice treat and following the steps covered here, you can teach your dog to lie on the ground on command in no time. As your dog gets used to this command, you can gradually remove treats from his training as described in previous tricks.

Up next, we look at how you can train your dog to give you a kiss.

Trick 5: Give Me A Kiss

Difficulty: Basic

What you will need: Peanut butter or cream cheese and treats

Amount of time needed: Around 5 minutes, 2 to 3 times in a day

Would you love to get a kiss on your cheek from your dog? If so, then you are in luck. This section will provide you with steps you can follow so that you can teach your dog how to kiss you. Once you are done covering it, you will be able to get your dog to kiss you any time on command!

Contrary to what you may believe, teaching your dog to give a kiss is not that complicated if given the right guidance. That said, read on the following steps to find out.

Step 1: Make sure your dog is hungry

Firstly, ensure that your dog is hungry. Why, you may ask? Because when your dog is hungry, he or she tends to be more motivated. A hungry dog will respond better to a food reward. As such, you will not have a hard time convincing your dog to respond to the next step.

Step 2: Smear cheese or butter on your cheek

Secondly, apply cheese or butter on your cheek. Up until this point, we have discussed training your dog using treats. This trick is a bit different. Although we could refer to butter or cheese as a treat, in this case, it tends to work better than ordinary treats that you may get. Cheese or butter is very specific to this trick.

Step 3: Call out to your dog to lick the cheese off your cheek

Thirdly, call out your dog and signal him or her to lick the cheese or butter off your face. Normally, dogs kiss by licking someone's face, so the point of this step is to get him or her to do that. As you call out to your dog, it is time to start issuing the command "kiss." Later on, as your dog gets used to the training, he or she will start associating the word "kiss" with kissing you.

Step 4: Give him or her praise and reward.

Fourthly, praise your dog for responding appropriately. Every time your dog performs something you liked, giving him or her praise reinforces the behavior. Your dog will understand that he or she performed as expected and will likely do the same in the future. After giving praise, reward with treats.

Step 5: Reduce the lure and reward

As you keep following the steps above for a number of days, say five, your dog should start getting a hang of it. From this point onwards, you can start gradually reducing the rewards you offer him or her. You can also reduce the amount of cheese or butter that you apply on your face. Keep doing this to the point where you can get him or her to kiss you without expecting anything in return.

Congratulations, you have now trained your dog to kiss you.

In summary, getting a dog to kiss you is an amazing trick to teach your dog. This chapter has shown that you can do this by primarily applying a lure such as butter or cheese on your face and getting your dog to lick it. As you do this, use the word "kiss" every time and your dog will in the future do it when you give it this command.

Were you expecting anything complicated, sorry to disappoint. Now let us move on to the next trick in line, training your dog to stay by your side.

Trick 6: Stay By My Side

Difficulty: Basic-Intermediate

What you will need: Some treats

Amount of time needed: Around 30 minutes a day

Have you seen one of those dogs that pull on the leash, roaming all over the place and cause a lot of trouble to their owners in a walk that was supposed to be peaceful and calm? It's an annoying scene isn't it? Perhaps it even happens to you when you take your dog out for a walk. Well, worry no more. This trick is going to fix that problem for you.

In this trick, you will learn how to train your dog to stay by your side whether you are walking or standing. This command is also known as the heel command, and will be the primary focus of this trick. After teaching it to your dog, you will have a much obedient dog that gives you peace during your walks.

Step 1: Put your dog on a leash

Restricting your dog's movement with a leash is the first step towards teaching this trick. You need complete control over your dog's movement; otherwise, you won't accomplish anything meaningful in the first stages of your teachings.

Step 2: Go to a calm and quiet place and acquire a heel position

The next step is that of finding a quiet place with fewer distractions. This is important so that your dog has fewer things competing for his or her attention. Once you have set up and ideal environment, you can get started by standing with your dog next to you in a heel position. A heel position simply means that your dog is standing directly beside you, especially on your left, although your right side is still fine.

Step 3: Offer your dog a treat and start walking

Now, you can give your dog a treat so that you get his or her attention and start walking. This is merely an attention grabber so that the rest of the steps you take become easier. Many times than not, your dog will do his or her best to do the things you want once he or she knows what is in it for him or her. And this is why treats are so instrumental to training dogs. After you offer your first treat, take the leash in your hand and start walking.

Step 4: Start issuing the "heel" command

As you start walking, start using the heel command as a way of beckoning your dog to come over next to you. Remember, the goal is to make your dog associate this command with walking beside you. So, the earlier and the more you repeat this command, the better.

Step 5: Reward your dog with a treat and a compliment

Your dog will start making an effort of keeping up pace with you. Every time your dog gets by your side, offer a treat as well as a compliment such as "good boy" or just "yes". You will need a handful of small treats because with this trick, you will be doing this quite often. So, once you have offered a treat and praise, continue walking.

Step 7: Issue an authoritative command and turn around

As you do this, you will inevitably run into instances when your dog tries to get ahead of you. If your dog does this, simply stop and issue the command "heel" in an authoritative tone and simple turn around and begin walking in the opposite direction.

This will send the message to your dog that he or she did something wrong which will prompt him or her to move in the new direction and try to keep up with you.

Step 7: Issue another treat along with a praise if he catches up

If your dog moves in the direction that you have taken, and catches up with you, offer him or her another treat and a reward for being a good dog. Repeat these steps over and over for a few yards as you walk your dog.

Step 8: Vary directions and introduce distractions

As time goes by and you start noticing a follow through in your dog's obedience to your heel command, you can start making the lessons more dynamic and real. For instance, you could try changing directions as you walk and only offer a treat for instances when your dog responds accordingly. You can also introduce new environments that have distractions so that your dog learns to be obedient in all types of situations.

Step 9: Remove the leash

If everything is running smoothly to this point, it is time to remove the leash from your dog. You want your dog to keep a heel position even during times when its movement is not restricted, so you need to teach him or her how to do that. The best way to this is to begin alternating periods of putting him or her on a leash with periods without a leash. Then, gradually work your way towards walking your dog leash-free as you notice his or her consistency.

Step 10: Gradually remove treats from the lessons

Now to the final step, if your dog starts showing consistency by walking by your side, it is time to start practicing without treats. Once again, start alternating periods of treats with periods of no treats. If your dog responds to well to both situations, you can keep reducing the number of times you offer treats until you remove them out entirely from your walks. At this point, you can be certain that your dog has successfully learnt the trick.

Teaching the heel trick is a slightly advanced exercise and may take more time than anticipated. This is in part due to the fact that some dogs learn faster than others. So if your dog is taking time to learn, it is important that you move according to his or her pace. All in all, if you keep persisting, your dog will eventually learn.

Now let us move on to the next section of intermediate tricks.

Intermediate

Now that we are done with the basic tricks, it is time looked at intermediate tricks as well. These tricks are relatively simple but more involving than the basic ones. They may take more time and effort for your dog to grasp. This is because they involve more steps than the basic tricks.

Trick 7: Speak

Difficulty: Intermediate

What you will need: A toy or a delicious treat

Amount of time required: Around 10 minutes a day

Another useful trick that you can teach your dog is to speak on command. Speaking in this case simply refers to barking. Apart from being a cool trick to impress friends and family, teaching your dog to speak on command, could benefit you in a number of ways. One way it will do so is by alerting you on potential intruders, visitors or impending danger.

Another advantage is that is that you will be able to control your dog's barking behavior. As we will see in the next chapter, you can actually train your dog to be quiet as well. A skill like this can help you get rid of bad barking behavior. There are many other advantages besides these, but my main focus will be on showing you how to teach your dog to speak. So let's get to it.

Step 1: Select the most appropriate reward for your dog

The first step involves selecting a reward for your dog. This could be your dog's favorite toy or a treat. In my experience, I have always found that a delicious treat works better. Nevertheless, dogs are anything but the same. So you should select one base on how well you know your dog.

Step 2: Trigger the barking by exciting your dog.

The next step involves getting your dog to bark. Again, this step will depend heavily in how well you know your dog. You could try showing him or her, a favorite toy and then hiding it behind you or having a friend knock at the door. Personally, I have found that a friend knocking at the door tends to work. You can try that in case you have no clue.

Step 3: Start rewarding your dog for barking.

Once your dog begins barking, then you know that you are on the right track. The next step to take at this point is to simply reward the behavior. As always, this involves handing your dog a favorite toy or a delicious treat. This is meant to make your dog start associating barking with getting a treat.

Step 4: Give a name to the behavior

Now that you have taught your dog to bark in expectation for a treat, it is time to introduce the command. Introducing a command is what will ensure that your dog will do exactly as it is told. To do this, simply say the word, "speak" or "talk" just before your dog begins to bark. Over time, your do will start associating barking with this command.

One thing to keep in mind is that as you issue the command; make sure you use the same voice and tone.

Step 5: Give out the command without trying to excite your dog in any way

Now it is time to try giving the command "speak" and wait to see if your dog responds by barking. If your dog barks after you issue this command, give it a treat as well as praise. Repeat this step for 10 minutes every day until your dog gets used to it.

Step 6: Gradually remove the reward from the training.

Finally, if you have gone through the steps above and your dog has responded well, it is time you started giving out commands without giving out a reward to your dog. The best way to do this is to gradually ease your dog into this by giving out orders with treats and failing to give treats at times.

As time goes, you can reduce the number of instances in which you offer treats until your dog gets used to it. At that point, you can safely assume that your dog has successfully learnt the trick.

Now that you know how to teach your dog to speak on command, let us look at how you can teach your dog to be quiet.

Trick 8: Quiet

Difficulty: Intermediate

What you will need: A few treats or a favorite toy

Time needed: Around 10 minutes a day

In the previous chapter, we looked at how you can train your dog to speak or bark on command. But then, how do you get your dog to be quiet once he or she starts barking. It can be really annoying to have your dog get started on a barking frenzy only to realize that you have no way of making him or her shut up.

Once again, there is a trick that you can teach you your dog that can help you accomplish this. This chapter will cover the steps that you can take so that you can train your dog to be quiet on command.

Step 1: Make your dog start barking

This is the first step towards training your dog to be quiet. If your dog has already learnt the "speak" command, you can use it at this point to make him or her start barking. If you haven't trained your dog yet on the speak command, you may want to revisit the previous trick and follow the steps there or simply perform an action that will excite your dog and make him start barking.

Having a friend ring the doorbell or knock at the door is one good way to do this. You can even try faking barking sounds of your own and see if your dog responds to that.

Step 2: Show your dog a treat to make him or her stop barking

If your dog starts barking after carrying out *step 1*, it is time to take out a treat or your dog's favorite toy and show it to him or her. You can even try bringing it close to your dog's nose. This should get your dog's attention and make him or her stop barking.

Step 3: Give the command "quiet"

Just before your do becomes quiet, give out the "quiet" command. You want to use this command at this point so that your dog learns to associate it with keeping quiet. You

can come up with any other word for this command as you
wish as long as you stick with it for the long term.

Step 4: Hand your dog a treat once he or she keeps quiet.

As always, you have to reward good behavior from your dog.
This is where this step comes in. At this point, if your dog
becomes quiet, acknowledge that by giving him or her, the
treat or the toy. On top of that, make sure you also praise him
or her. A simple "Good boy or girl" should work just fine.

Step 5: Start waiting longer before you give the treat.

If you have covered the steps above for some time, your dog
should have grasped the concept pretty well. Now it is time to
start delaying your treat. Do this by not giving the treat to
your dog immediately you issue an order. Wait for longer
before you give your dog the treat.

If your dog responds accordingly, by going quiet immediately
you give the order and stays patient until you hand over the
treat, you can move on to the next step.

Step 6: Gradually remove the treats from your training

The next step, which also happens to be the last, involves
gradually removing treats from the training. Do this by
alternating periods with treats with periods of no treats, until
you can safely issue an order to your dog without him or her
expecting any treat. Then you will be sure that your dog has
learnt the trick.

We have looked at how you can get your dog stared on speaking and how to make him or her go quiet. These two skills may look simple but they form a great part of an obedient dog. A dog that barks when it is supposed to and goes quiet when it is told is so fun to have around. Hopefully, this and the previous tricks have shown you the best ways to do that.

But what if you wanted to teach your dog to roll over? Read on to find out.

Trick 9: Roll Over

Difficulty: Intermediate-Advanced

What you will need: A few treats, a soft spot for your dog to roll over

Time needed: Around 20 minutes, a day

The next exciting trick to teach your dog is the "roll over". Getting your dog to roll over on command is an impressive trick that you can show off to your friends and family. However, here is the deal: this trick is slightly advanced. As such, it may take more time and more work for your dog to learn it. However if you are willing to put in the work required along with a fine dose of patience, then you will get results in due time.

This chapter will show you steps you can take to teach your dog to roll over. Let's begin.

Step 1: Make your dog lie down

The first step towards teaching your dog this trick is to make him or her lie down. Before you can teach your dog to roll over, your dog needs to first know how to lie down. This is why I decided to discuss the lie down trick in the previous trick before getting to this one. In case you haven't taught your dog the lie down trick, I encourage you to visit the previous trick and follow the steps there before you can move on with this chapter.

Step 2: Hold a treat close to your dog's nose

With your dog lying down on the floor, squat and bring a treat close to your dog's face. Take care not to hand it over to him or her yet. Close your fist or hold the treat firmly with your fingers if you suspect that your dog may snatch.

Step 3: Move the treat around and issue the command "roll over".

The next step involves moving the treat around. As you hold the treat in your hand taking care not to hand it over to your dog just yet, move it around over your dog's head so that he or she follows it. Make sure to move it along a path that makes your dog to roll over as he or she follows it.

As you do this, issue the command "roll over." Make sure you say it in a voice that is friendly and clear. This is meant to make your dog associate this action of rolling over with that phrase. In the future, when your dog hears it, he or she will tend to perform the action of rolling over.

Step 4: Give the treat to your dog along with praise

Now it is time to reward your dog for acting accordingly. A treat in this case serves the purpose of sending the message that your dog performed accordingly. On top of that you should praise him or her. Pat your dog gently on the head and say, "Good boy or girl."

The job from this point onwards is to keep repeating the steps covered so far for a number of days, say four before proceeding to the next step.

Step 5: Issue a reward and praise only after your dog rolls over

As you repeat the steps thus covered, your dog should start expecting a reward and a compliment every time you issue the command 'roll over'. If your dog isn't, continue repeating the steps until you notice him or her responding to the command. After you take note of this, start giving a treat and praise only when your dog rolls over when you issue the command.

Step 6: Gradually remove treats from your training.

Once your dog is responding well to your command, it is time to start fading out treats from the training to the point where your dog just rolls over and expects nothing in return. As usual, start by minimizing the number of times that you offer treats and then slowly work your way to the point where you are literally offering no return. Once you get to that point, your dog will have successfully learnt the "roll over" trick.

As you have seen, the process of training your dog to roll over is not particularly difficult. The only thing that you will have to invest more is the time and dedication you put to it. As I've said before, your dog may take more time to learn this skill, so it helps to persist with a lot of patience. As time goes, your efforts will pay off and your dog will effortlessly roll over on command.

With that covered, let us now move on to the next exciting trick, teaching your dog to crawl.

Trick 10: Crawl

Difficulty: Intermediate

What you will need: A treat

Amount of time needed: Around 10 minutes, 2 to 3 times in a day

Another exciting trick that you will learn to teach your dog is crawling. While this can be a fun and exciting to show off the skills that your dog has to your friends and family, it also serves an important purpose. In a way, crawling is an exercise. Therefore, by teaching it to your dog, you will be working his or her muscles and therefore making him or her healthier.

In this trick, we will be looking at definite steps you can take to teach your dog how to crawl. So let's get to it.

Step 1: Get a nice spot for your dog.

The first step you should take is that of finding an ideal place to train your dog. Remember, not all surfaces are conducive for this trick. So try finding something cushier. A good example would be a smooth or carpeted floor. You could also take him or her out on a grass field.

Step 2: Start with the sit command and then get him to lie.

This is one of those tricks that would require your dog knowing a few tricks upfront. In this case, your dog needs to have mastered the "sit" as well as the "lie" command. In case your dog hasn't learned these commands yet, kindly go over the previous tricks that we have discussed and train your dog first before you can proceed with this guide.

If your dog already knows them, then get him to lie down by first issuing the "sit" and then later on the "lie" command.

Step 3: Get some treats

After your dog lies down, get some treats in your hand. As always, you will always need treats for most of the training. The point is to reward your dog in an effort to reinforce a certain behavior or action.

Step 4: Lower the treat ground level and beckon your dog to move forward.

Now, get closer to your dog, squat and hold a treat at ground level a few steps from him or her. As you do this, start giving off the command, "crawl." You could even try patting on the floor as a way of beckoning your dog to start crawling.

Step 5: Reward and praise your dog

Once your dog sees the treat and reads your body language, he or she will start moving towards you, trying to get to the treat. If your dog crawls in an attempt to reach you, reward him or her immediately. If he or she tries to stand, gently push him to a down position with your hand and continue giving the command crawl.

If your dog is having trouble with this step, sit on the floor, bend your knee and place your foot flat on the ground creating a small arch using your leg. Now the goal will be to get your dog to pass through this arch. Once again, entice him with a treat and give the command "crawl." If your dog successfully passes through the arch you have created, reward him with a treat and lots of praise. Repeat this step until your dog can crawl without you putting out your leg for him or her.

Step 6: Gradually increase the distance.

As your dog gets better at crawling after going through the steps above for a number of days, start increasing the distance that he or she must cover. Take a few steps back each time until your dog is comfortable covering a considerable distance.

Step 7: Slowly remove treats from your training.

If you have been carrying out the steps above with success, your dog should have understood the trick as well as the command fairly well. Now it is time to start slowly working towards eliminating treats from the training program. Alternate periods of treats with those of no treats to the point where you won't need them anymore to get your dog to crawl.

In conclusion, crawling is an amazing trick that is impressive as well as healthy. This is because it works the muscles of your dog. As such, sometimes your dog may get tired and sore during the training. This may end up slowing down the process. Nevertheless, you need to understand that this is a slightly advanced trick that may take more time for your dog to learn.

We will now look at another trick i.e. jumping into your arms.

Trick 11: Jump Into My Arms

Difficulty: Intermediate

What you will need: A treat

Amount of time needed: Around 10 minutes, 2 to 3 times in a day

Imagine this: You are hanging out with a bunch of friends in your house talking about how amazing your dog is and one of them dares you to pull an amazing stunt. You then call out to your dog, who then shows up very quickly. After you issue the command jump into my arms, your dog springs up onto your lap in excitements and relaxes at once. Would you want that? It's an amazing trick isn't it?

Fortunately, you are holding in your arms a book that is going to show you how to turn that dream into reality. Read on to find out how.

Step 1: Get some nice treats

The first step in this process will involve acquiring some nice treats that your dog enjoys. You will need a number of them because they will serve as an incentive to get your dog to perform the jump to your arms.

Step 2: Get seated on a chair

The next step involves getting seated on a chair. This will be the starting point of your training. In the beginning, before your dog gets used to the jump, you will need to provide a modest height for your dog to attempt to jump on. The height of chair serves that purpose.

Step 3: Hold up some treats on your hand and give the command

This steps involves making use of the treats you acquired in step one to entice your dog to make a jump. To do this, simply hold out a treat so that you get your dog's attention. Then speak out the command word. You can use anything you like for this purpose. In my case, I prefer just saying "jump onto my arms."

As you speak out the command, it helps to signal to your dog by either stretching out your arms or patting on your lap.

Step 4: Help out you dog in case he or she has problems

If your dog is having a hard time figuring out what you are trying to communicate, it helps to give out a clue. Do this by carrying of your dog from the ground and placing it on your laps. Then repeat the steps from the second one.

Step 5: Reward your dog for responding appropriately.

The next time you repeat the steps and your dog jumps on your lap reward him or her immediately by handing over a treat. As you do this, give him or her lots of praise to reinforce the act. Dogs love praise, especially from their owner. This helps your dog learn much faster.

Step 6: Increase the height.

Once your dog is carrying out the jump consistently a number of times, it is time to raise the challenge by increasing the height. You can do this by sitting on a table and following the previous steps. If your dog responds well, you can try performing the steps while standing. Given enough time and patience, your dog should be able to do it eventually.

Step 7: Gradually remove the treats from your training

Now that your dog is effortlessly jumping into your arms once you give the command and stretch out your arms, it is time to consider phasing out the treats from the training.

Just like we have discussed in the previous tricks in this book, you should start reducing the treats gradually to the point where you will not need them at all, at which point you should assume that your dog has successfully gotten the hang of it.

Given these steps, training your dog to jump into your arms, essentially involves holding out a treat as an incentive and beckoning him or her to jump into your stretched-out arms. As your dog gets used to it you then take out treats from your lessons. It may take more time but with persistence, your dog will eventually learn it.

This trick concludes our discussion of intermediate tricks. In the next section, you will learn more advanced dog tricks.

Advanced

Now that we have covered basic as well as intermediate tricks, it helps to throw in a few advanced tricks into the mix as well. Unlike the tricks that we have covered up to this point, these ones tend to be more challenging. Also, the steps involved are more elaborate. As such, they may take more time and effort from you and your dog for successful learning to take place and therefore more patience is required.

Trick 12: Fetch

Difficulty: Advanced

What you will need: A treat and a toy

Amount of time needed: Around 10 minutes, 2 to 3 times in a day

In this chapter, we will look at how you can train your dog to fetch an item. Not only is fetching an amazing trick to teach your dog, but also a game that would be fun to play with your dog. The fetch trick works like this, you throw an object, say a ball a few yards from your dog and he or she rushes to get it. Then he or she brings it back to you.

Now, many people mistakenly think that all dogs instinctively know how to do this. But the fact of the matter is most dogs do not know this trick unless they were taught somehow. Your dog may be okay with running and collecting an item but he or she may fail to bring it back to you. The goal of this trick is to teach you how to train your dog to do it the right way.

Step 1: Put your dog in a sitting position

This is the starting point of your training. Before anything else can be done, get your dog to be in a seated position. Why is this important? Because you want your dog to be calm and relaxed. You do not want to begin your training with your dog trying to jump and trying to snatch the toy from you before you even attempt to throw it (in case you are training with his or her favorite toy).

Step 2: Get some treats and a favorite toy

The next step you need to take is that of acquiring some treats and your dog's favorite toy. The treat is for rewarding the desired action while the toy will be the item your dog will fetch. You can get whatever toy your dog fancies. But for the purposes of this book, I will use a ball as an example.

Step 3: Give the toy to the dog so that he or she can smell it

After getting your dog's favorite toy and treats, bring the toy (in this case the ball) close to your dog's nose so that he can sniff it. The goal in this is to make your dog become comfortable with the toy you are holding. This is especially important if you brought a new toy for this purpose.

Step 4: Grab your dog's interest.

Now it is time to make your dog interested and excited. The best way to do this, if you are holding the ball, is to bounce it consistently on the floor. You should read excitement in your dog's body language. For instance, wagging the tail and breathing heavily while sticking out the tongue are good signs of interest.

Step 5: Throw the toy a few yards from your dog.

Once you are sure that your dog is excited, it is time to throw the ball. Throw the ball a few yards from where you are standing. Your dog should take notice of this and rush to grab the ball. As your dog rushes to get the ball, you should be giving the command "fetch". You could also try saying,

"Go get it!" Any phrase you come up with is fine as long as you remain consistent with it.

Step 6: Congratulate the dog and call him or her back.

If your dog picks up the ball, you should reward him or her with praise. This reinforces the message that he or she performed the desired action. After you congratulate your dog, you should immediately start calling him or her back. The training isn't over until your dog brings the toy back to you. So call him/her my by name and beckon him/her to come back.

You could try patting on your thighs, or calling out his name in an excited voice so that he is encouraged to come back.

Step 7: Give a command to release the toy.

Once your dog comes back, it is time to signal him or her to drop the toy. You could try spreading out your arms to see if he or she understands this. As you do this, give a command that you hope he or she will associate in the future with this action. An example is "give it" "release" or "drop it." If this doesn't work, take out a treat and show it to your dog. Your dog will be prompted to release the toy so that he can get the treat. If your dog does this, you have accomplished your objective.

From now onwards, you should repeat these steps over and over for as long as is necessary. You could try throwing the toy a little farther and reducing the number of times you issue a treat. Gradually work your way to the point where your dog sets out to fetch the toy and brings it back without expecting a treat.

In conclusion, fetch is an amazing trick that allows you to exercise your dog and also develop a good bond with him or her. It can also be nice to show this trick to other people. If you diligently follow the steps provided, your dog will be master at fetching in no time. Now let's get to the last trick in this book, "teaching your dog to search for an item."

Trick 13: Search For An Object

Difficulty: Advanced

What you will need: A treat and a toy, or some other object

Amount of time needed: Around 10 minutes, 2 times a day

Have you seen one of those classic movies in which a very talented dog tracks a missing person or a missing object? Imagine how amazing it would be if your dog was able to do the same. Dogs have a very sharp sense of smell. With a little know-how, you can turn your dog's amazing talent of sense of smell into a very important skill. The goal of this trick is to show you how to do that. By the time you are done working though the content in this trick, your dog will be an expert at tracking simple hidden objects.

So let's get started.

Step 1: Get a toy or some object that you would like your dog to track.

This is the first step in the process of training your dog to track things. You could get a toy that your dog is very fond of playing with. You could also try getting an object that has a strong smell. This could be your T-shirt that smells of you or your hat. The bottom-line is to find something that your dog can easily relate to and that has a strong smell.

Step 2: Show the item or toy to the dog.

Next, call up your dog and make him or her get seated in front of you. Then, show him or her, the item or toy that you would want him or her to find later on. This is meant to make your dog get familiar with the item or object you are holding. At this point, it would be useful if you tried to play around with it so that your dog generates some interest in it.

Step 3: Give the item or toy to the dog to smell it.

The next step involves you bringing the item close to the nose of your dog so that he or she can sniff it. Remember, dogs track things by smell. So this step is critical to the success of your training. By doing this, you will be giving him or her, an idea of what he or she will be looking for.

Step 4: Restrict your dog's movement and hide the object.

After giving your dog the item to smell it, restrict his or her movement. You could simply do this by putting him or her on leash and tying it around a pole or something else. You need to do this so that your dog cannot follow you to the spot where you will hide the item. After you restrict your dog, hide the object. At this point, try hiding it somewhere that is easy to figure out, such as under a piece of clothing.

Step 5: Release your dog and give the find command.

After hiding the object, release your dog off the leash and give him or her, a command to go and get the item. Try giving a command such as "go find 'item name'". Do this in a voice that sounds happy and excited. If your dog sets out to find the item, cheer him or her up. If he or she finds it, give him praise.

If your dog has trouble with this step, try finding the item with him or her. And then repeat the steps above a couple of times. Over time, your dog should start grasping the concept you are trying to drive home.

Step 6: Reward with a treat.

Once your dog retrieves the hidden object, you can try calling him or her back in case your dog isn't bringing the item back to you. Once he or she gets back with the item, reward with a treat and praise.

Step 7: Repeat

If your dog goes through the steps covered successfully, it is time to start repeating the procedure. Go over the above steps time and time again. As you do this, try hiding the item in different places. Also try hiding the item in difficult to find places as well. As you do this, try minimizing the instances in which you offer treats.

In the end, your dog should be able to track a hidden item using his or her sense of smell once she is given the command. He or she should be able to do this without expecting a treat too. Since this trick is advanced, your dog may not get a hang of it immediately. However, just like other advanced tricks we have discussed, if you invest enough time, effort and patience, your dog should be able to do this flawlessly.

Read on to find out how you can train your dog to dance on hind legs.

Trick 14: Dance On Hind Legs

Difficulty: Advanced

What you will need: A treat

Amount of time needed: Around 10 minutes, 2 to 3 times in a day

Training your dog to dance in a circle on his or her hind legs is another unbelievably amazing trick to teach your dog. In addition to being entertaining to watch your dog perform such a trick a trick, dancing can be another way of keeping your dog healthy because it helps him or her burn off excess energy and work out his or her muscles.

Like other advanced tricks, this one can be a little more difficult to teach your dog especially if he or she is a slow learner. However, if you have the right guidance, like the one provided in this book, it becomes a lot easier. Therefore, a lot of patience and diligence is required. So let's begin.

Step 1: Get some nice treats

I've said this many times and it bears repeating, nearly every important trick you teach a dog will require that you employ the use of treats. Treats serve as an important incentive for the desired action as well as a way of reinforcement. So, as usual, make sure you get a number of treats that are your dog's favorite.

Step 2: Lure your dog

The next step is that of luring your dog. You can do this by holding the treat in your hand and bring it close to your dog's mouth. This will grab his or her attention immediately. Your dog will start following your hand in an attempt to get the treat. Now you are ready for the next step.

Step 3: Move your hand around in a circle.

Now it is time to start moving your hand around in a circle. Do this while your hand is still at ground level but do not hand the treat over to your dog just yet. This is meant to prime your dog for the next step that will involve standing. After completing a circle movement, hand over the treat to your dog and take out the next one and get ready for the next step.

Step 4: Raise the treat and give the command

This step is the core objective of this trick – getting your dog to stand on its hind legs. So raise your hand as you hold the treat. Your dog will be eager to get the next treat and so he or she will begin standing on its hind legs as he or she tries to reach it. As you do this, give the command. This could be anything. I prefer, "dance around"

Step 5: Reward and praise

Reward any attempt that your dog makes of standing on his or her hind legs at this point. Your dog may not do it perfectly in the beginning and that is okay. You have to understand that this is an advanced trick and so perfecting it requires a lot of practice. So reward your dog and give him or her lots of praise so that he or she will be prompted to do better next time.

Step 6: Raise the treat and move your hand in a circle.

As time goes by and you have repeated the steps above a number of times, it is time to make the training a bit more aggressive and challenging. Move your hand around in a circle in the same way you did in step 3. As you do this, do not forget to give the command. Also, do not hand over the treat until your dog completes going round in a circle while standing on his or her hind legs.

You could even try using one command for anticlockwise spinning and another different for the clockwise direction.

For instance, you may say, "dance right" or "dance left." A good practice would be to use a different hand for each command. Amazingly, your dog is capable of learning the difference if you take enough time. Once he or she does that, then you know that you are closer to your end goal.

Step 7: Start gradually reducing frequency of tricks and hand signals.

As always, training is never complete unless your dog is capable of performing it without expecting a treat or following your hand signal. Instead of just quitting giving him or her, the treats or the hand signal all of a sudden, a better way would be to gradually ease him or her into getting used to it. Slowly reduce instances of rewards and signals to the point where he or she performs the trick without expecting anything. Then you will be sure that your dog has completed the training.

In the end, training your dog to dance on his hind legs comes down to two things, luring your dog with a treat which is held up above the ground and guiding him or her to move around in a circle with your hand. If you can do this repeatedly while giving the required command, your dog should be able to perform it after some time without needing much assistance.

Now, let us take a look at the final trick in this book, skateboarding.

Trick 15: Skateboarding

Difficulty: Advanced

What you will need: A treat

Amount of time needed: Around 20 minutes, a day

Are you somebody who loves to skate during your free time? Could you imagine your favorite dog, showing up and joining you in this fun activity? Teaching your dog to skateboard is one of the most unbelievable tricks that could go on to prove how smart dogs really are. Just imagine you and your dog skating across the street and everyone turning around to watch this unbelievable scene.

If you imagine the incredible popularity this can bring you, training your dog is the ultimate trick that you can teach your dog. Fortunately, you are holding in your hands a book that can give you step by step instructions on how you can train you dog to skateboard.

Step 1: Introduce your dog to the skateboard

The first step is that of introducing your dog to the skateboard. Your dog needs to get used to seeing the skateboard and stepping on it before he or she can learn anything advanced. So, place the skateboard on a surface that will restrict movement such as a carpet on grass.

Let your dog smell the skateboard and become excited about it. Also take care that the skateboard does not move. If it does, your dog may become scared of it and this may make teaching the rest of the lessons take longer.

Step 2: Reward your dog if it places on of his or her paws on it

The second step is that of rewarding your dog for expressing interest in the skateboard and even stepping on it. So watch your dog carefully at this point. If he or she places one of his or her own paws on the board, immediately shower him with lots of praise and a treat. Doing so will send the message to your dog that he or she has done the required thing which will make him or her want to do the same or even better next time.

Step 3: Start using the command word

As your dog begins the first few phases of training by even placing one of his or her own paws on the board, you should start using the appropriate command word. It is often a good practice to do this early on in the training so that your dog associates the command with the act of stepping on the skateboard. Some good commands to use are, "step" or "get onboard." You are still free to invent your own command word.

Step 4: Start moving the board around.

The fourth step involves moving around the board. Do this without your dog aboard. The point of doing this is to make your dog gets used to the idea that the board is a moving thing. Remember not to shove the board in the direction of your dog, or you risk scaring him or her off, which has the potential of disrupting the flow of learning.

Step 5: Reward and praise the next time your dog gets on board.

After introducing your dog to the idea of moving board, it is time to give him or her, another chance of getting onboard a stationary board. If he or she responds by getting onboard, reward him or her with lots of praise and treats once again. However, this time reward your dog only if he or she gets on board with all four legs.

Step 6: Push the board slightly with your dog on it.

Now it's time to push things a little further. Instead of having your dog stand on a stationary board, you need to make things a bit riskier by moving the board around a bit. So, give the skateboard a slight push with your dog on it and wait to see his or her reaction.

Step 7: Reward your dog for staying onboard.

If your dog stayed onboard after moving the skateboard even if for a few seconds, you should reward him or her. Remember, this is an advanced trick. Do not expect your dog to learn everything overnight. You should reward and reinforce every small step he or she takes along the way. Expecting too much of your dog in the beginning is just being plainly unfair. As time goes by, your dog will begin to understand that he or she needs to stay onboard for longer, at which point you should move to the next step.

Step 8: Get your dog to push the board

You have gone through the steps above repeatedly and your dog is showing progress by staying onboard the moving skateboard even as you push it for longer distances. Congratulations. But the journey isn't over yet. How do you get your dog to push the board by him or herself? This is what this step accomplishes.

This is the trickiest part and depending on the level of your dog's intelligence, it may take more time than anticipated. Command your dog to get onboard the skateboard on a gently sloping surface. Then, take one of your dog's paws with your hand and place it on the ground. As your dog tries to get the paw back onboard, the energy should push the skateboard forward. As you do this, give the command word again. Saying "skate" should work perfectly at this point.

Once again, reward your dog for this step with lots of treats and praise.

The key from this point is to keep repeating this step for as long as it takes until your dog learns to do it without your help.

Step 9: Gradually remove treats from your program

If you have been following the steps above with consistency, over a period of a month or so, your dog should start getting better at skating. Once you notice this, you should start removing treats slowly from your training to the point where you will no longer need them. At that point, you will be certain that your dog knows how to skateboard.

To finish off, this chapter has gone over the steps you can take if you want to train your dog on how to skateboard. In a nutshell, this chapter has shown that all you need to do is simply introduce your dog to the skateboard, reward him or her taking interest in getting onboard, moving the board around a little without him onboard, moving it around with him onboard and finally teaching him or her to move the skateboard by him or herself.

Although training your dog to skateboard can feel like a long short, if you take on it with persistence, patience and determination, with time your dog will eventually do it.

Conclusion

We have come to the end of this book on tricks you MUST teach your dog.

In this book, we have looked at basic, intermediate as well as advanced tricks that can be taught to your dog. Truth be told, dogs are often smarter than you could imagine. By investing your time and energy in teaching your dog the tricks covered in this book, you help bring out the smart side of your dog, which can help you communicate, relate and bond well with your dog.

The tricks covered in this book are not all there is to it. They are just a tip of the iceberg, but all the same, they are a good start. There are a lot of tricks out there that can be taught to your dog. What I encourage you from now on, is to invest in more books like this one which can offer you more guidance on the world of dog training. By doing so, you will be doing you and your dog a huge favor.

I want to finish off by thanking you for choosing to buy this book and taking the time to read this far.

Now is your turn to take action!

Do You Like My Book & Approach To Publishing?

If you like my writing and style and would love the ease of learning literally everything you can get your hands on from Fantonpublishers.com, I'd really need you to do me either of the following favors.

1: First, I'd Love It If You Leave a Review of This Book on Amazon.

2: Get Updates When I Publish New Books

Visit my Amazon page and subscribe to receive notifications whenever I publish new books.

3: Grab Some Freebies On Your Way Out; Giving Is Receiving, Right?

I gave you a complimentary book at the start of the book. If you are still interested, grab it here.

5 Pillar Life Transformation Checklist: http://bit.ly/2fantonfreebie

PSS: Let Me Also Help You Save Some Money!

If you are a heavy reader, have you considered subscribing to Kindle Unlimited? You can read this and millions of other books for just $9.99 a month)! You can check it out by searching for Kindle Unlimited on Amazon!

Printed in Great Britain
by Amazon

72451665R00045